DISCOVERING

GOD

"TO KNOW HIM & SHARE HIS LOVE WITH OTHERS"

INTRODUCTION

This is a collection of Meditations. Food for thought.
Seeds of ideas offered in words and pictures —
the purpose of which is to discover in Jesus' life,
his words and actions, the Personality of God.

"I and my Father are one:"
from birth to death Jesus & his Father were a unit.
So it may be presumed that in his human life
Jesus was a perfect reflection of the nature of God.

We search in the Gospels to learn how we humans
should live .... what we should be like....
I want to discover what the Gospels say about God.

"When you have seen me you have seen the Father"
said Jesus.

PART 1. Son of God — PART 2. Son of Man

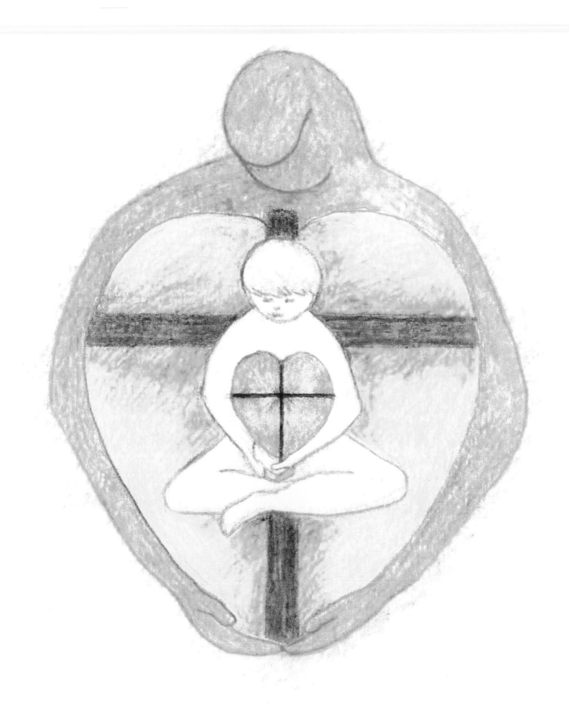

"Jesus said:

'I am in my Father,
              & you in me,
                    & I in you."

PROLOGUE – Part 1.

GOD
IS   invisible, mysterious, absolute Reality,...
      at the heart of all things that exist.
The Creator leaving the mark of his Personality in
all things he has made – (as does anyone who creates) –
In Jesus God made himself visible in a human body,
& thus he revealed his Personality, his Spirit, in a
tangible form that could be discovered & experienced
more easily by human beings.
Within Jesus we can learn what God is like, and
we can see that God is present within all human
experiences & feelings. In our own Life, within
our thoughts & feelings, we can find God for ourself.
It is not that he is outside us, observing us from
afar but, in a way we cannot understand, that he
is present within every experience, every feeling
that we have. It is mystery. In some mysterious
way we can be aware of his actual Presence
within our Self, part of all we are & all we do.
This experience of relationship will not be forced
upon us – but if we allow it & open our mind we
can become aware of something within our
Consciousness which is more than our own Identity,
our own Personality.   This is the Personality
of God present in us. God in us & us in God.

In Jesus God reveals HimSelf –
In Jesus we can discover what God is like –
In Jesus we can find our true Self.

GOD IS CREATIVE

First & foremost God is the Creator Life-source.
"He created everything and there is nothing exists
that he did not make"... (St. John. 1:3)

He is present within his creation.

We who are made as an image of God are ourselves creative. In every thing we make we
express something of ourself _ Similarly in
every thing that exists we see something of
God: his creative power, his aliveness & beauty.
We wonder at the minute things seen only
under a microscope... at such a tiny creature
as a flea which has the same organs & body
systems as a dinosaur or an elephant.
We can wonder as much at a feather as
at a forest tree; at a pebble as a mountain;
at a water drop as at an ocean wave; at a
firefly's light as at sun, moon & stars.
  "To me the meanest flower that blows gives
thoughts that lie too deep for tears" (W. Wordsworth)
  Well may we be puzzled by the seeming
harshness of nature... asking what this says
about God?... surely: that God is beyond our
understanding! God will always be MYSTERY.
The creator must be greater than the creation.
If it were not so he would not be worshipped
(you do not worship your equal!) This is a very
humbling thing _ & yet he communicates
with us, loves us, guides us, helps us.

9

"SPIRIT OF GOD FREE AS THE AIR

GENTLE AS IS A DOVE

LIKE AIR GOD IS EVERYWHERE

GOD IS SPIRIT

"God is spirit & everyone who worships Him will worship Him in spirit and in Truth" (St.John 4.23)
"Just as you can hear the wind but cannot tell where it comes from or where it will go next, so it is with the Spirit" (St.John 3.8)

Spirit has no tangible form or visible appearance. It is the essence, the truest reality of a Person's Identity. As it is of God's Identity.

The wind is a wonderful illustration of this. Wind is air that is moving: breeze or hurricane. We cannot see the wind, but we can hear & feel it, and see what it does. We use words to describe it: words such as 'roaring, whispering, howling' for its sound; mighty, powerful, gentle, carressing for its feel. We also use the image of a gentle dove for spirit.

How, then does this imagery describe God? Certainly not as a sort of super human Being! God is something uniquely, invisibly "else"

So how can we physical mortals experience God? He acts within our perception of our Self.... unforeseen thoughts drop into our mind — our feelings or reactions may suddenly change. To recognise God we need to open our inner awareness to a possibility beyond physical Self. It is a conscious decision taken in trust to set our minds into "neutral" — no thoughts — or to send a cry for help out beyond ones Self.

This "beyond", this invisible experience, is where God-Spirit meets our spirit, where we "know" God in a mysterious but very personal & real relationship.

11

GOD IS LOVING

"God loved the world so much that He gave His unique Son ....." (St. John. 3:16)

Love, as St Paul describes it, is patient, generous, kind, humble, unselfish, unbiased, forgiving, and unfailingly constant. (1 Corinthians. 13:4-7)

God's love is the epitome of true Love .... It is probably beyond our full comprehension! From the Bible it seems that God can't not love anyone. He may not like what we are, or approve of what we do — but His Love is as constant as the air we breathe — & as essential for Life. It is more than mere liking or desire. His Love is everlasting. It is the source of our ability to love.

To know we are loved regardless of whether we accept or reject His love, is so amazing that it leaves one speechless! How can one express a response to such a huge giving? One can only accept it & receive it into ones inner Being without trying to understand it or to explain it.... even less trying to describe it.

In His Love God will do anything to enable us to experience Him, to draw us into a relationship with Him — It was for this that He created us! He desires this more than we realise ... He even accepted human torture & agonising death to demonstrate the lengths His Love would go to in order to defeat the evil powers that would separate us —

His Resurrection was & is the victory of His Love over Evil. Love stronger than Death —

13

GOD IS JOYOUS

"He (Jesus) was filled with the joy of the Holy Spirit". (St. Luke 10:21)

"You will be filled with my joy" - (St. John. 15:11)

In the past the Church has given a picture of a rather glum, demanding, straight-laced God; but Jesus had a good sense of humour — as seen in some of His parable stories.. And He reflected the Personality of God.

Joy is more than happiness. The Dictionary definition is: intense gladness; extreme delight; great pleasure. Does God feel joy as we do?... Since we are "made in His Image — a reflection of His Nature — He must be the Source of our joy. This is a wonderful thought which we can reflect into our World. Joy brings awareness of God into our lives. When we feel Joy—full our inner Being is sharing God's Joy. Jesus felt a deep Joy of Spirit when the Disciples returned from a mission tour having seen the power of Evil overcome in people's Lives. Maybe God's Joy is greatest when someone turns to Him, & when the Evil Power is defeated.... "There is joy in heaven when one sinner repents" (St. Luke 15:7)

Joy is God's reaction to Victory over temptation & evil. "For the joy that awaited Him Jesus endured the Cross" (Hebrews 12:2)

God rejoices and shares His Joy with us!

GOD IS UNIVERSAL

"Foxes have dens and birds have nests, but
I have no home of my own" — (St. Matthew. 8.20) —
"I am with you always". said Jesus. (St. Matthew 28.20)
After Jesus left His family home he became a
wanderer; sleeping and eating wherever He
was invited in —   This represents how God
is freely present everywhere in His Universe.
Each of us is surrounded by His Presence — But
He will only become involved in our lives when
we invite Him in. He never presumes upon us!
Because He is everywhere He is always
with us whether or not we recognise Him,
respond to Him, or ignore Him. This
should be for us a comfort and strength.
We do not have to clamour for the attention
of a remote, uncaring deity...
Our Father-like God is within a thought's reach
wherever we are, night or day — A thought
alone is enough. Words are not a necessity.
Even as we think or speak He is responding.
This may be difficult to accept or to take in
because we are restricted by Time and Space.
God created both of these, so is not limited by them.
We cannot possibly understand His
universality (omni-presence) — We do not
need to! Just be amazed, awe-struck,
thankful that He is immediately available
throughout His entire created universes.
For you — for me — for everyone.. here ..& now!

17

GOD IS POWERFULL

Power is the authority to carry out ones intentions & the ability to overcome any opposition — The Power of God is spiritual, unbeatable but not violent — Its effects are seen in the physical realm of Humanity — This power was revealed in Jesus by His Life: helping people to relate to God in a new way. He said "I am the Way" (St. John 14:6) Jesus revealed God's power in many ways. Most of those recorded are of healing of the body or the mind — He also used His power to restore those pronounced dead. And where people had succombed to the power of Evil He had authority over the 'demons', to drive them out..."In all things the Lord's healing power was upon Him" (St. Luke 5:11) because He was "full of the Holy Spirit" (St. Luke 4:14) God's power in the world of Nature was also shown by Jesus:— turning water into wine;... multiplying loaves & fish;.. calming raging sea storms; & walking upon the sea waves. Today God's power is seen both through prayer & the medical professions...."Those who believe shall use my authority" (St. Mark 16:17)   So in spite of all the Evil in our World, God's power will never fail, but He uses it as He wills. Not as we Will! Never-the-less He does not over-rule the Free Will He has given us.
'Yours is the Kingdom, the Power, & the Glory for ever.."   It is awesome!.

GOD IS PEACEABLE

Jesus seems to present us with a contradiction!
"My peace I leave with you, my peace I give you"...
then later: "I come not to bring peace but a sword."
(St. John 14:27, & St. Matthew 10:34)
Does an explanation lie in what sort of peace
Jesus meant? He did not come to sweep away
war & cruelty & fear & suffering. To do that
would be over-riding our Freedom to choose the
Good or Evil for ourselves. He also said: "In the World
you will have tribulation, but I have overcome the
world." (St. John 16:33) Follow His ways & seek to do
good, & we shall discover that inner, spiritual
peace that He possessed even when He suffered.
With this Peace comes the Sword of the Spirit to
overcome the dark things in Life. Then however
much we are troubled by events, or suffer at
the hands of others, or are stressed or depressed,
if we turn to Jesus, abandoning our own efforts,
we shall find a strange sense of calm pervades
us.. relaxing our body & releasing our mind
from anxiety, giving us hope and courage to
endure what we cannot avoid. The Peace that
"passes understanding". This peace we pass to other
people when we greet them at the Eucharist.
with the words: "The Peace of the Lord be with you"
Jesus greeted His Disciples, appearing after His
Resurrection, "Peace be unto you" (St. John 20:19).
He offers us too His Peace... shall we stop our
struggling and receive it?

"MERCY is the sympathising, pitying, goodness of GOD"

GOD IS MERCIFUL & FORGIVING

This aspect of God's Nature is probably one that most personally affects us — Created to be a reflection of the nature of God, we fall far short of His perfect goodness. Yet this amazing Creator is never failingly merciful towards us. Jesus tells us: "Be merciful as your father is merciful" (St. Luke 6:36) ... He has unending compassion for our failures, pities our stupid, obstinate independence, and has sympathy for our sufferings. Jesus said "Your sins are forgiven .... the Son of Man has authority on earth to forgive sins" (S. Matthew 9:3&5) But why would God forgive us? Even in His own agony of Crucifixion Jesus prayed for the perpetrators as they killed Him: "Father forgive them, they know not what they are doing"— Mercy & forgiveness are natural to God, but still we need to ask for & accept them even as we recognise & repent our faults. This is humility for we shall never 'deserve' these gifts! Jesus told a woman taken in adultery (which was a capital offence) "Go on your way and sin no more" (St. John 8:11) He understood all her circumstances, as He knows ours, so He had mercy & gave her a new start. Sin forgiven. Maybe God's greatest demonstration of His mercy was indwelling Humanity in Jesus; showing us that temptation, & the Evil in our World can be overcome by His power, & His mercy & forgiveness are always there for us.

GOD IS COMPASSIONATE

Compassion, pity, sympathy: Jesus expressed all these toward people He met_ For example "Jesus wept" when He saw His friends' grief at the apparent death of their brother (St. John. 11:35). He was "moved with pity" for two blind beggars. (St. Matthew 20:34)_ He felt compassion for the crowds of sick & needy who came to Him for help. (St. Matthew 9:36) He was moved to tears over the disbelief of the people of Jerusalem (St. Luke. 19:41) He felt deep sympathy for those people who were struggling with the heavy burdens of their lives (St. Matthew. 11:28-30) & He offered them rest in Himself. All our pains are shared by God. He feels for us just as we feel for the pain of those we love_ The greater the love relationship the greater the shared pain_ God is the Source of all Love, & we cannot imagine the extent or nature of His suffering with us. Sometimes in our deepest suffering we may feel that God is remote & detached; maybe even uncaring? But compassion & pity are not necessarily only, or even best, expressed by actions_ Rather it is knowing that someone cares about us, that we are not forgotten, alone, but someone is with us, understanding how we feel... this is what really helps_ And this is what the Invisible Presence of God gives us_ At the centre of a hurricane, the "eye of the storm" is a stillness, a calm space. God is that central place in our spinning emotions, our whirling trouble & pain. In Him we can find a calming place. He cares.

GOD IS OUR JUDGE

What is Judgement?   We think of a Court Judge or Magistrate judging criminals... But what about judgement of competitions or of quality?_ Assessment not condemnation _ God knows everything about us. "Man looks on the outward (obvious), God looks upon the heart".... (1 Samuel:11.7) Man sees actions _ God sees motives & causes. God looks at Good & Evil. As Creator He is responsible for the existance of both. Is this contradictory? Or can it be explained by the fact that we experience things by opposites: hot/cold, dark/light etc.?... Good opposite to Evil. But since these are incompatable, at the final judgement good will be drawn to God & evil be destroyed. Jesus taught in metaphors such as the division of sheep (good people) from goats (evil people). The sheep go to eternal life with God. The goats are separated from God, even destroyed (St. Matthew:25.32) This seems to be very harsh, even a merciless judgement... Or could it be saying that each of us will be assessed as individuals? God knows the good & bad in us, & our difficulties. "He does not crush the weak or quench the smallest hope"(St. Matthew:12.20). So in-so-far as we have believed in God & tried to serve Him we will be safe, & sure of fair judgement. (St. Matthew:24.45& chap 25) Jesus is both Judge and Saviour. We should not fear His Judgement. Just live as He has shown us. God is just.

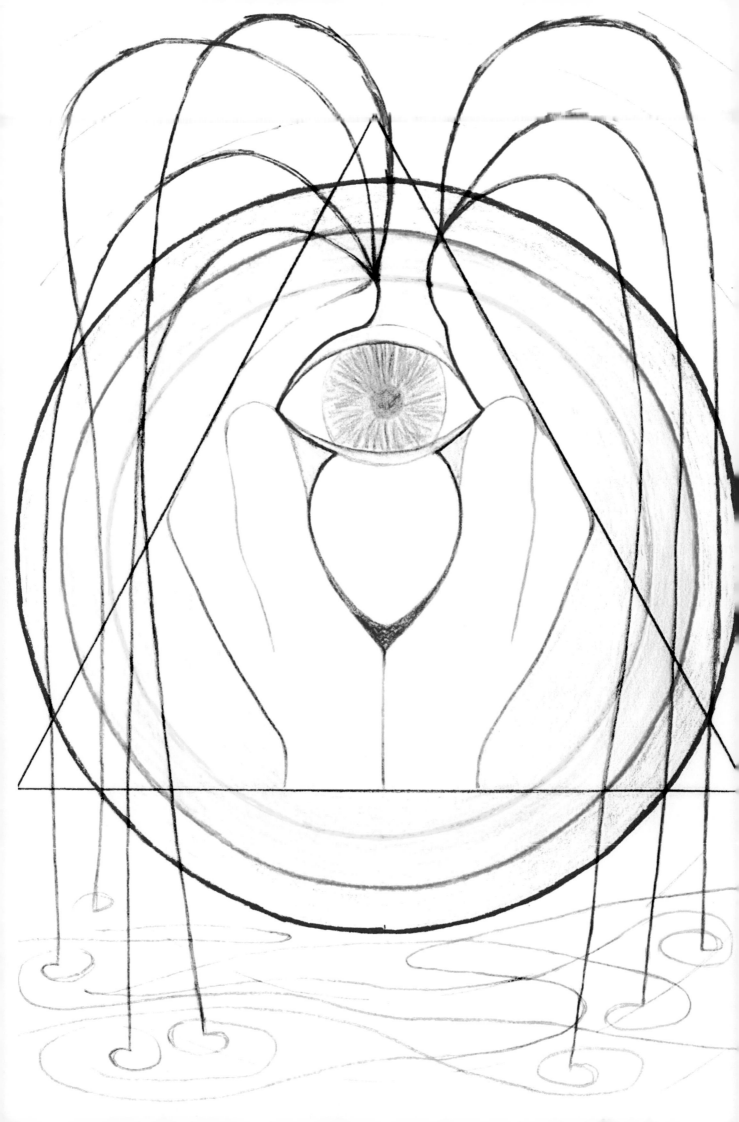

GOD IS WISE

He is the source of all Wisdom — True Wisdom
is not intellectual ability, nor academic knowledge.
It is not being quick-witted, nor clever. Wisdom
cannot be learnt. Perhaps it is the intrinsic
awareness of what is best in any situation —
It will not necessarily be what human limitations would consider best, because God has
the capacity to know everything about all
'Present' & 'Future' circumstances. So Wisdom
may allow the apparently worst scenario
because through it the best may be attained.
Jesus, at His trial, showed how this can be true.
(St. Matthew. 27: 11-14., & St Mark: 14:60-62 & 15: 2-5, & St. Luke 23: 7-9,
& St. John 18:19 — 19:16) — Jesus only replied to questions
if it was appropriate, but not when it would have
made no difference to the outcome. Sometimes
Wisdom just remains still & silent. In His wisdom
Jesus knew this. He was master of the situations
which, although they led to suffering & death,
ultimately attained His world-changing Victory.
The whole of Jesus' healing & teaching ministry
exemplifies the varied wisdom of (the Son of) God:
evident if one looks closely at His motives...
It can be seen when the Jews brought to Him
a woman taken in adulterous acts. (St. John 8. 3-9)
A test situation about His attitude to moral Laws.
By word, by silence, by action He demonstrated
the true meaning of Wisdom: Law-abiding &
merciful! Throughout the Gospels we can
discern & wonder at God's true Wisdom.

29

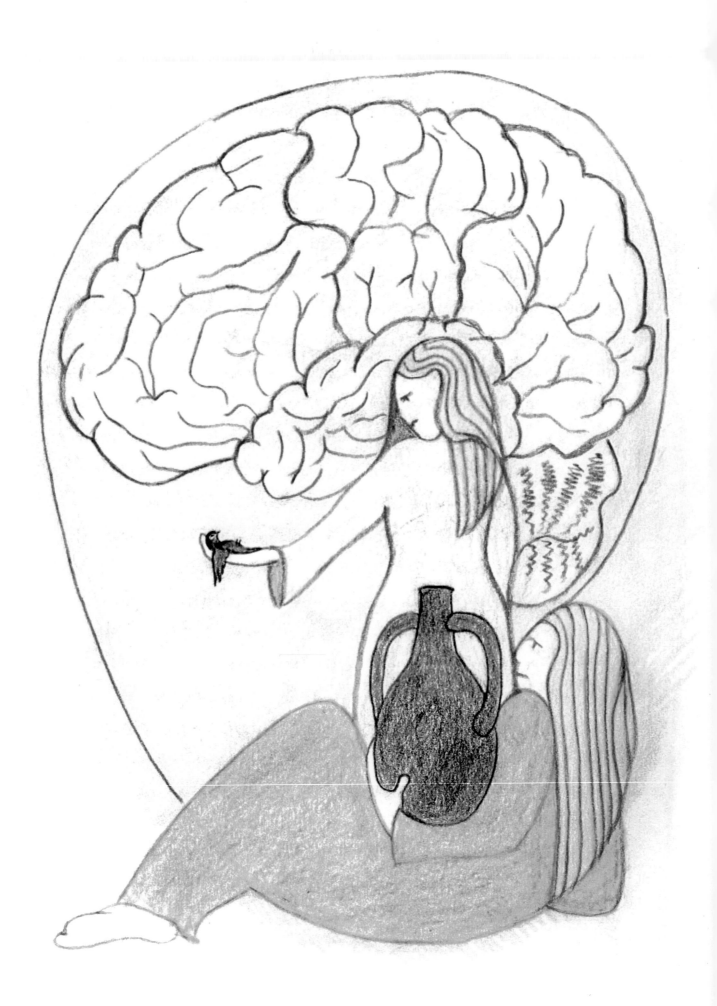

GOD IS ALL-KNOWING

"Oh Lord you have examined my heart and know everything about me" ___ "You are thinking of me constantly": (Psalm 139)
It is impossible to envisage this ability to know all about everything & everyone at the same time! Some people have a sporadic intuitive sense - Jesus had this ability in its full capacity. He knew what people were thinking (St. Matthew. 16:32, & 22:18)(St. John. 1:40) (St. Luke. 6:8) — He knew all about human nature (St. John. 2:25). He showed the woman at the well that He knew all of her past life (St. John. 4:18). He also knew the future (St. Luke 19: 41-44)
Jesus shows how God knows all about each of us: the troubles we have been through, & what has motivated our actions, be they from good intentions or bad. He knows our exact individual details & appearance (St. Matthew 10:30)
He also is aware of the smallest occurences in all His universes — even when a sparrow dies! (St. Matthew. 10:29) ___ Such all-embracing knowledge is totally beyond our comprehe- -nsion. This could be scary; but only if we want to hide a guilty conscience! It should really be immensely reassuring. We are so greatly cared for, & loved as unique individuals — Never ignored, never deserted. We never have to 'put Him in the picture' before conversing with Him. He knows.

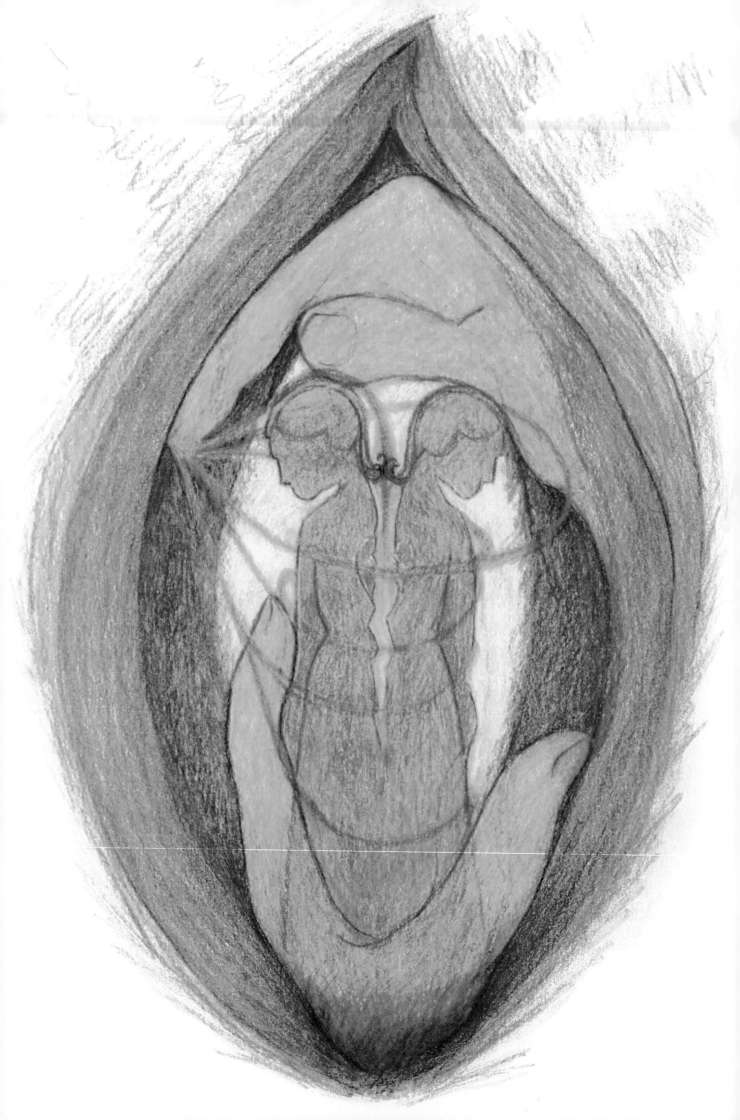

GOD IS OUR HEALER

Healing is not just curing the body. It is making people totally well in spirit, mind &/or body. Making them "whole" as Jesus said. (St. Mark 5:34) (St. Luke 8:48 & 17:19) – Sometimes He healed a purely physical condition such as blindness or deafness. Sometimes it was an illness such as leprosy Sometimes mental or psychological disorders. "He healed every kind of sickness & disease.... if they were possessed by demons, insane or paralized – He healed them" (St. Matthew. 4:24/25). Jesus healed spiritual wounds as well – forgiving the guilt & sin when these were the root cause, (St. Luke 5:20). Jesus loved to give back to people the health that was God's design & desire for them. And nowadays?   Yes – God is still our healer. Our bodies are created to be whole, & they have a natural capacity of self-healing. But sometimes it needs the help of medication. God also heals through the ministries of doctors, dentists, surgeons & psychologists. And through the channel of prayer as a direct route of His healing power....... But what of illness & injury which does'nt heal? Maybe a healthy, balanced Personality (the Soul) is of greater importance to God. It is sometimes apparent that God does great things through those who are not healed. This is one of the mysteries about God which our human minds cannot solve ! Healing may not be perfect fitness. It may also be perfect ability to serve God: regardless.

GOD IS LIFE-GIVING

Jesus said: "I am.....the Life "(St. John. 14:6)
"To all,...Life He giveth'—'In all Life.....He liveth"(Hymn)
God is the only originator of Life; "Life in all
its fullness"(St. John.10:19): Living; moving; thinking; being.
We Humans sense that Life does not end when
we die. The physical body does die. Is it the Personality that lives on? "The dead shall live &
know Jesus. Those who believe have passed
from death to life"(St. John.5:26/27). Jesus said: "I can
give you this Life-eternal"(St. John. 5:40). We cannot
understand how this Life-Force functions, but
we can discover God-the-Giver-of-Life: Life
now & Life everlasting.—Death is therefore
the transition from one way of life to another.
An alteration not an ending.—Yet God warns
that there are those whom He cannot accept.
This is the result of their chosen unbelief;
it is not His desire. We are told that for
them it will be eternal existance of sorrow and
spiritual agony (St. Matthew.25:41-43). We should heed this
warning though we do not know what it means.
God gives what we call the Gift of Life to all
his creatures and plants. But to His human
children He also gives a never-ending spiritual
existance — eternal Life beyond death.. So
it seems that the nature of our everlasting
life depends on our attitude toward God, &
toward goodness (if we do not know God). Perhaps it
is our motives for how we live now that will live on.
God gives us Life ...we choose how to live it.

"you will
hear
a word
behind
you:
'This is
the way,
walk
in it'"

(Isaiah 30)

GOD IS OUR GUIDE

We have free-will to choose how we live our Life.
But to live it in harmony with God and His
purposes we need His guidance, & His help—
Even Jesus in His human form had to receive
guidance from God-the-Father....We read that
He often went off alone to talk with Him:
"He went into the hills to pray" (St Mark 6:46). Thus He
paused before reacting in difficult situations:-
before the first miracle, at Cana (St. John. 2:1ff)...;
before responding to Lazarus' death (St. John. 11:1-43),
before passing judgement (St. John. 8:34),...agonising
in the Garden of Gethsemone (St. Matthew. 26:29)
If Jesus needed guidance... we certainly do!!
We have His assurance that He will "guide our
feet into the way of peace" (St. Luke 1:79) But not
necessarily to the end of violence... God guided the
Wise Men to safety (St. Matthew 2:1), but Jesus to the Cross.
If we accept that we need God to guide us, then
how do we seek & recognise His guidance?
Firstly we ask for it. God does not force His
way upon us— Then we have to have an open
mind... God will guide us by different means at
different times— He may put thoughts into our
minds;...He may use other, reliable peoples' advice;
circumstances may open up opportunities,...
We may find guidance in reading, or in dreams.
God-the-Spirit will "guide" you into all Truth" (St. John 10:13)
You just have to "ask & it will be given to you:
seek & you will find" (St. Matthew. 7:7).
"God knows what you need before you ask" (St. Matthew. 6:8)!

GOD IS THE WAY

Jesus said: "I am the Way....". (St. John 14:6)
      and: "Follow Me". (St. John 12:26. & others)
Besides meaning a pathway, we talk about
the way in which we do things— To follow
someone also means to imitate their methods.
So Jesus' words could mean: "I am living in
the way God wants for me. Follow my example".
We cannot exactly copy His Life. Our world
& societies are greatly changed from His times.
His example lies in the MOTIVES behind His
words & actions... All He said & did came
from His love for people. He saw people as
individuals. He responded to them regardless
of nationality, sex or status. He listened
to them; did what He could to heal them;
to comfort & encourage them; to show that
God loved them all. In the same way each
person needs & has a right to our respect &
attention & care. His love will be seen by
others when we follow His way of living.
There might be a certain anxiety in doing
this because Jesus also said: "Take up your
cross & follow Me"_ (St. Matthew. 16:24). The cross
was for Him His destiny: (the only way for
God to show how far His love will go to meet us.)
Our calling is to accept our own destiny,
whatever course our life takes, an easy way
or hard. Then, within our circumstances, to
try to imitate His example of love by being
loving as the motive of all we do & say.

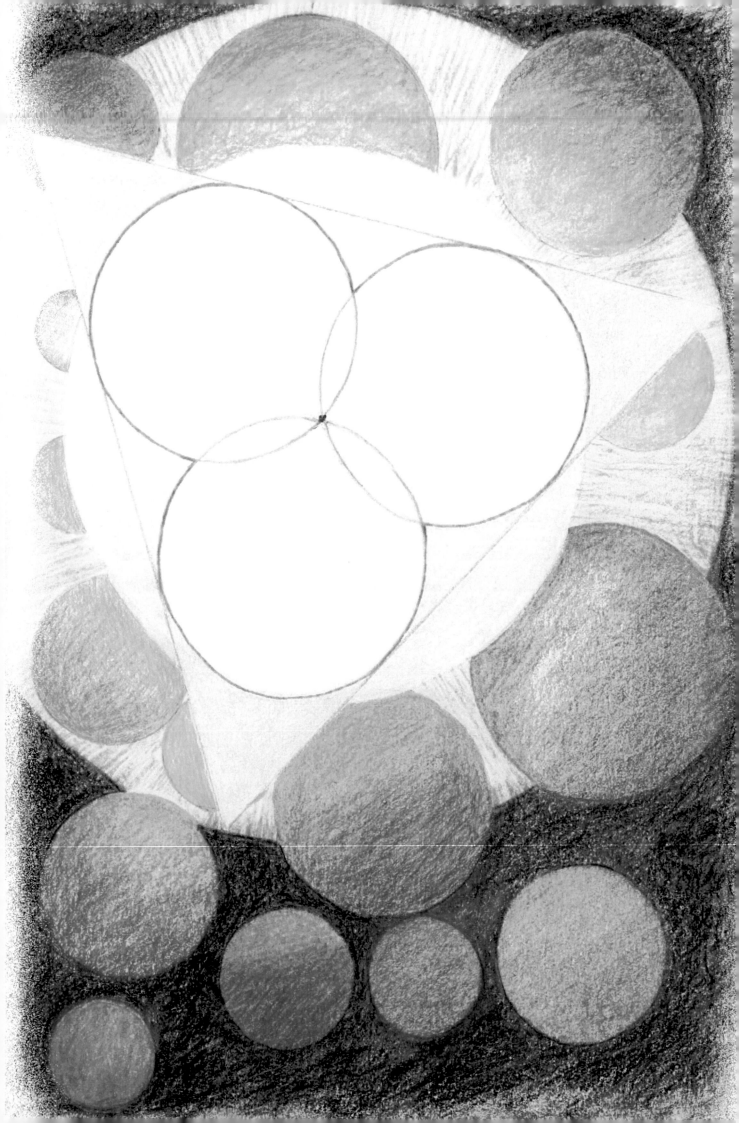

GOD IS THE TRUTH

Pilate asked Jesus: "What is Truth?" (St. John 18:38)
One definition says that Truth is 'positive, unde-
niable (irrefutable) fact'. Another says it is someone who is exactly what they appear to be... no
hidden agenda.... speaking & behaving with
total openness & honesty — Truth is Love expressed
without counting the cost.
God, being the Source of all things, is the Source
of Truth. Thus Jesus is the Truth visibly expressed.
He said: "I am... the Truth" (St. John 14:6) — Nothing that
he said or did was without love. Even His anger
was a response to peoples lack of integrity & love.
His parables are illustrations of Truth put into
practice, & we are to discern from them what
He is telling us about living in Truth.
By word & example He is giving us an idea
of what Truth is. — "I came to bring Truth to
the world" (St. John 18:37) — "I say what I am
told to say by the One who sent me, and
He is Truth" (St. John 8:26) Also Jesus speaks of
the Holy Spirit, who comes to help us, as
"The Holy Spirit who is Truth ...shall guide
you into all Truth" (St. John 16:13) And Jesus
assures us that "if you live as I tell you
you will know the Truth" (St. John 8:31)
In the Anglican Confession we admit " the
Truth is not in us." We who should be a
reflection of God's nature mar that reflection
by our sins. We are a blurred image..... So
What is Truth? It is disturbing! It is
absolute Goodness & Love. Only God is like that.

Those doing right
come gladly
to the Light

(St. John 3:21)

THOSE WHO LOVE DARKNESS STAY AWAY FROM THE LIGHT_ (St. John 3:19 & 20)

GOD IS THE LIGHT OF THE WORLD

Jesus said:" I am the light of the world".(St.John 8:12)
"His life is the light that enlightens all mankind"
(St.John.1:4) In Him God enligtens us to see the love
& goodness of God's true nature. The true light
"to shine on everyone" (st.John.1:9) so that each
one may choose to reject or recognise Him_
Sometimes it is hard to see any light when
circumstances are dark, but " His life is the
light that shines through the darkness, and
the darkness can never extinguish it"(St.John 1:5)
However appalling things are, or seem to be,
however Evil seems to have the upper hand,
if one looks closely there will be some sign of
goodness... Maybe as small as a smile, or the
touch of a kind hand, or even just an unspoken
unknown prayer...The light of love & hope
will be present somewhere _ "In all things
God works together, for good, with those
who love Him & obey Him". (Romans 8:28) Some
people may think the light has been extinguished
but it will alway show up somewhere. _
God cannot be destroyed. He is eternal.
But His goodness & love are only able to be
seen where goodness is acknowledged & love
is put into action _ That is like a
beacon to guide our way through Life.
Follow the light of God's love & goodness... do
good... be loving.... you will be reflecting His
Light into your world.

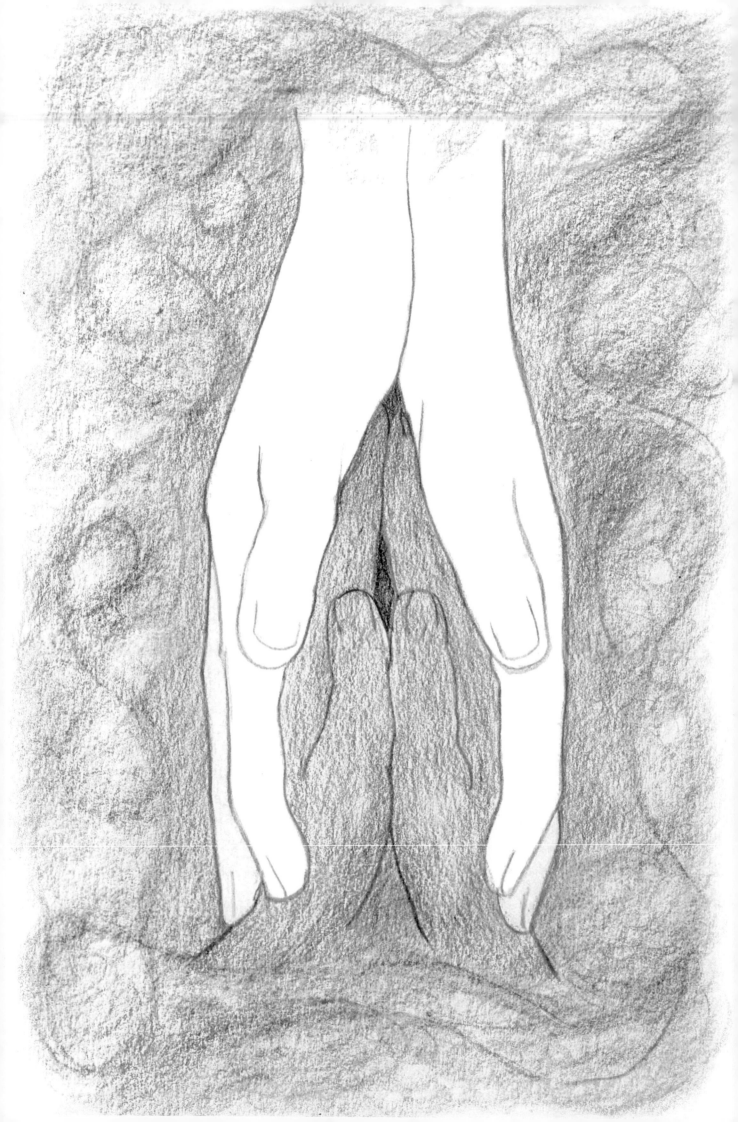

GOD IS REASSURING

This reassurance lies in the promise of Jesus's continuing Presence: "I am with you always" (St. Matthew 28:20) and in the promise that the power of the Holy Spirit would be ours after Jesus had completed His ministry on Earth: "I will send you another Comforter" (St. John 14:16) — In old English to 'comfort' meant to encourage ... to put courage into. "Do not be afraid of those who threaten you" said Jesus (St. Matthew. 10:26) He also reassured those who believe & trust in Him that their eternal Life is a certainty. (St. John 6:47). Even if our faith is uncertain, He will still be beside us, helping us. Sometimes we stupidly try to do things on our own iniative & relying on our own strength, but when we come to our senses & turn back to Him, Jesus reassures us: "I am with you always" (at all times) "even to the end of the World" (St. Matthew. 28:20) — Sometimes He may not seem to be close ... we may not 'feel' Him near us ... but this is a promise made by our God: & He does not break His word! He may not remove our problem, but He will encourage us to cope, & reassure us of His strength available to us. "Do not be afraid Just trust Me" (St. Mark 5:36) What more can we ask!

GOD IS SUPPORTIVE

When we are having a hard time God does not leave us to struggle on our own, or flounder in overwhelming circumstances. He offers His support with whatever we need in order to cope – But we have to ask for His help: even if only the words 'Help me lord'. This is because He wants a person-to-person relationship with us based on our personal decision – We must choose whether to struggle on too proud to admit our limitations, or whether to swallow our independence & allow Him to interact with us. Mutual love & respect. If He seems to be slow in helping it is because He will not mollicoddle us at the least difficulty. But He will never leave us beyond endurance. Jesus gave this kind of support in His ministry. When Mary of Bethany sat listening to Him while Martha was busy, He took Mary's side when her sister grumbled (St. Luke 10:38 & 42) After two of His healing miracles when the sufferers were being bullied by the Jewish authorities Jesus sought out the man to give him encouragement (St. John 5:14 & 9:35). And when Peter's fear was stronger than his faith – once when he was drowning, and later after Peter's denial – Jesus came to support & reassure. (St. Matthew 14:30/31 & St. Luke 24:34) God has not changed His policy. He is still on hand, & when we call to Him in our hour of need He will respond as is best for each of us.

You call me
"Master"
& "Lord"

I your Lord &
Teacher have washed your feet

feet that are dirty & sore from walking along dusty roads

(St. John 13: 13/14)

GOD IS GENTLE, HUMBLE & KIND

Sometimes Jesus showed that God will not
tolerate those who wilfully disobey or disregard
Him — but toward those who are struggling
He is gentle & kind. Jesus quoted the Old
Testament prophecy about Himself: "a bruised
reed He will not break & a smoking flax (wick)
He will not quench" (St. Matthew 12:20) If we have
the least desire to start afresh God will help.
"Wear my yoke & let me teach you, for I am
gentle & humble" (St. Matthew 11:29) In those days
a farmer would harness an experienced, older
animal with a young one to teach it how to pull
the plough. But God is also humble (strange
as this may seem!) He helps if asked but also
He will accept our right to reject Him — Another
illustration of His gentle nature was how Jesus
grieved over the obstinate disbelief of the Jews.
"O Jerusalem, Jerusalem how often I have
wanted to gather your children together as
a hen gathers her chickens beneath her wings;
but you would not let Me (St Matthew 23:27) Like the
caring of the mother hen God is longing to
protect all people — Too many try to struggle
on by ourself! When we reach the end of
our tether (or hopefully long before!) if we
stop our racing thoughts & our churning
emotions we can become aware of the
mystery in our mind that is that "Still
small voice of calm (1 Kings 20:12)
Regardless of status or race He is there for us.

GOD IS PROTECTIVE

Jesus told us to pray that God our Father would not "lead us into temptation," & would "deliver us from Evil". (St. Matthew. 6:13)_ If we ask for His protection He will back us up in our battle against Evil_ Jesus also gave us a parable of this: The Good Shepherd. In the East they did not use sheepdogs. The shepherd led his flock from the front, & they followed, trusting he would choose a safe way & would feed them & protect them. The shepherd protected his own flock, & would even die in their defence _ Their sheepfolds were a ring of stone walling with a gap entrance, but no gate. At night the shepherd would lie across the gap like a gate to fend off thieves or wild animals. (St. John. 10:1-16) _ The relationship between shepherd & sheep was very close. He recognised each sheep individually, and they knew the voice of their shepherd and would respond only to him _ You could not have a better illustration of the Christian's relationship with God. His intimate knowledge of us & desire to protect us from losing our spiritual way or being overcome by worldly values. Our trust in Him & obedience to Him is our only safe option among the secular distractions of life. Even in the "nighttimes" of Life God is still protecting us, even when it is hard to be able to realise this. And some find it harder than others.

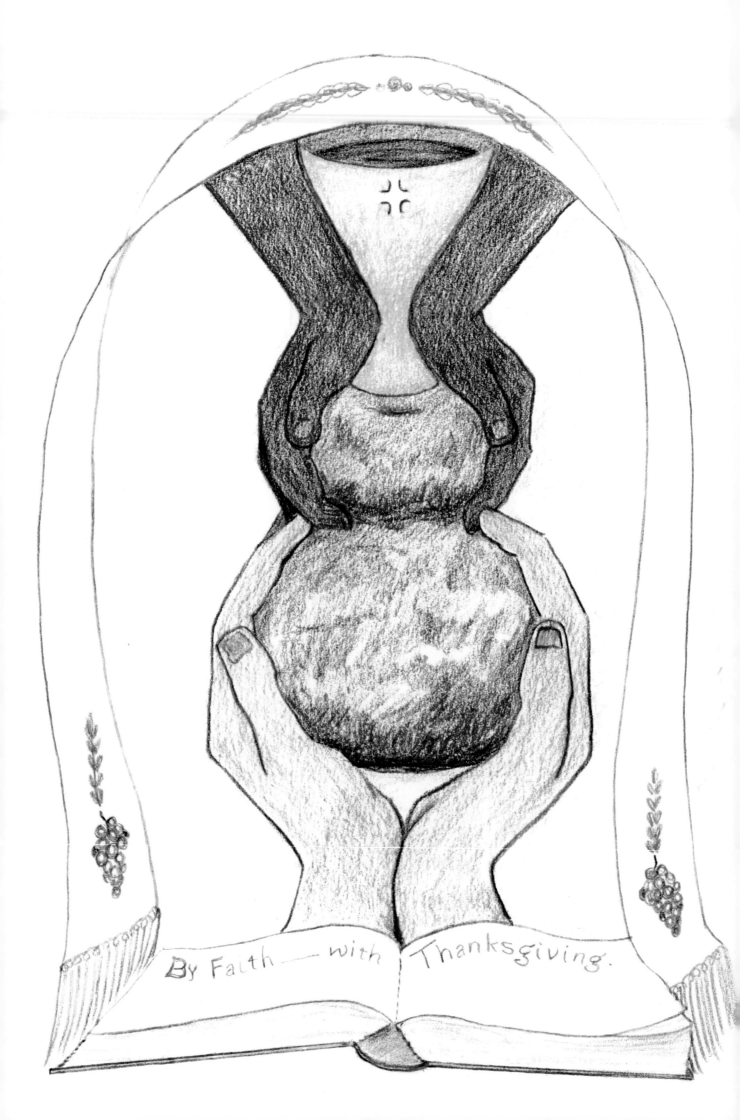

By Faith — with Thanksgiving.

GOD IS SUSTAINING

God provides the spiritual nourishment to sustain us on our journey through life. Jesus said: "I am the Bread of Life" (St. John 6:35) It is His Presence in our life that nourishes the development of our relationship with God. In studying Jesus' life we can learn how we are to sustain our life with & in Him__When we pray "Give us this day our daily bread" that is what we are asking for. (St. Matthew 6:11) Bread is the basic food of many people & the sustanance of God should be our basic desire. Jesus also called Himself the True Vine, & likens us to the branches. (St. John 15:1-8). The sap flows from the stem of the vine into the branches which can then bear fruit: the grapes... From the grapes comes the wine which nourishes & strengthens those who drink it. God's power flowing into our mind sustains & nourishes our spiritual life. Jesus is the Source of our spiritual nourishment... "Bread" & "wine" for the journey - for ourselves, & to share with others. Jesus gave us a powerful symbol of this which we re-enact in the Service of Holy Communion (Mass — Eucharist — The Lord's Supper) In an unbroken line from Jesus' hands at the Last Supper (St. Mark 14: 22/23) we partake of bread & wine, given from hand to hand. "This is my body given for you"... "my blood shed for you (St. Luke 22: 19/20)... "do this in remembrance of Me". In this way, & by prayer & Bible study God has provided our spiritual sustanance.

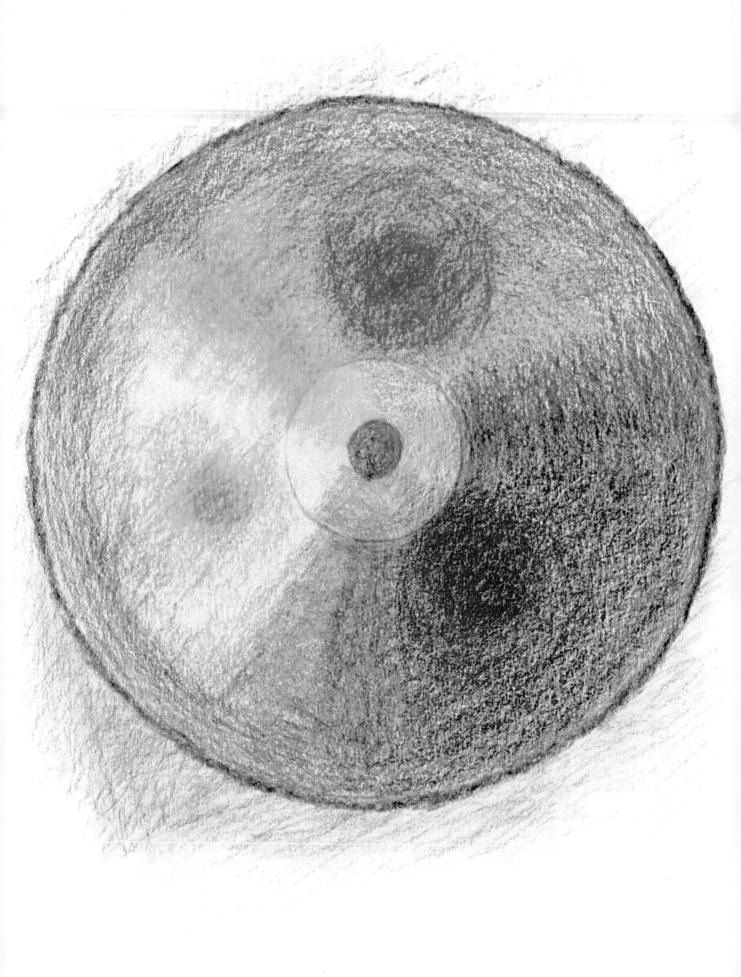

GOD IS ONE

When Jesus said "I and my Father are one(St. John.10:30)
He was expressing what seems like a contradiction.
Pagan religions saw God as several individual gods
with different areas of responsibility. The Jews
were the first to understand the unity of God.
But they seem to have seen Him as a super
human Being with human faults & virtues.
Then God revealed His true Self in human
form so people could experience the Reality.
"When you have seen Me you have seen the
One who sent Me"(St. John 12:45)_& "When you
have seen Me you have seen the Father(St. John.14:9)
After Jesus was crucified & His incarnate
revelation was completed, He remained
available to human experience, but not
visible. As the Holy Spirit of God(St. John. 14: 15-17)
"My Father will give you another.... He lives
with you now & some day shall be in you."
So although God is one Being He can be
experienced in three aspects_ This is not
difficult to understand. We ourselves are
comprised of several systems in one person.
We have our Minds_ our Bodies_ & our inner
Identity (spirit) Even our bodies contain
several systems: digestion, circulation,
respiration etc. Separate & inter-active.
We are made in God's image (Genesis. 1: 26)
God is Mind: the Creator, the Father-figure.
God is Body: Jesus, "Son" of God, revealing Him
God is Spirit: Holy Spirit, the invisible Presence.

HOLY HOLY HOLY
HOLY HOLY IS TO COME IS THE
HOLY HOLY LORD
IS THE AND GOD
LORD IS ALL
AND MIGHTY
WHO WAS

(from a Hymn)

GOD IS HOLY & ETERNAL

"From everlasting to everlasting" (Psalm 90:2) without beginning or ending.   And Holy:- perfect in every way — Timeless Perfection. Jesus said "Be perfect even like your Father in heaven is perfect" (St. Matthew 5:48) — God had said to the ancient Jews; "Be holy for I am holy". (Leviticus 11:45) ...... a tall order indeed!

We cannot achieve anywhere near to this unless we ask for & receive Holy Spirit to change & empower us.

God's holiness is eternal, as He is, It is virtually impossible to imagine anything that has no start nor finish — But for God to be all that we believe Him to be He has to be more than any Human Being. He is unique. There can be no 'creator' of God, since He is Himself the Creator of all that exists.—

When Moses asked God to give Himself a name God said. "I AM" (Exodus 3:14) Never "I was", never "I will be". God is the eternal 'Now'. We cannot understand. Only believe in Faith. Jesus applied the 'I AM' to Himself when He was challenged by the Pharisees during His ministry — & at His trial when challenged by the High Priest — For any person to use the Name of God for himself was blasphemy. Unless you were the Holy God Himself!

(St. John. 8:58 & 18: 5-6) also (St. Matthew 26:63-64).

(..impossible to portray..)

57

GOD
15

EPILOGUE

I have explored some of the aspects of the nature of God as seems to be revealed in what we know of Jesus-Son-of-God. But without doubt there are things that I have missed! In the Old Testament we read that the Jews seemed to have the image not only of a loving God but also of a vengeful side to His nature - Anger I can understand. But love & vengeance do not go together. So I have made no representation of a dark side of God - Yet all things are only recognised because of their opposite: heat & cold, high & low, cruel & kind etc. So there must be a dark side to the goodness of God. As Creator of Good He must also have created Evil in contrast - Yet this seems alien. But I can see no alternative source of Evil if we have only one Creator. It is in seeing evil that we recognise goodness, and vice versa. The goodness of Jesus shows up the evil of those who opposed Him & killed Him. Without the choice between being good or evil we would be puppets not individuals. There would be no choice in our relationship with God. It would seem that Evil is necessary!

I set out to discover in the Gospels something of God's Personality as He revealed Himself by becoming incarnate: living in human form. I have tried to express my thoughts in words & in illustrations - in a very personal way. It has been enlightening!

.....✝ESUS SON OF GOD

JESUS SON OF MAN......

THE LIGHT SHINES THROUGH THE DARKNESS & THE DARKNESS CAN NEVER EXTINGUISH IT —

JESUS

(St. John. 1 : 5)

PROLOGUE - Part 2

Jesus revealed the nature of God: Son-of God. He also revealed the best of human nature — Son-of God born of a human mother, He was also Son-of-Man - experiencing all the emotions of every human being. It is because of this that we know God shares our problems & our suffering as well as our happiness.

Feelings are part of our God-given nature; our response to the events we encounter. We can express them or bottle them up...They can control our life, or we can manage them.

By studying Jesus' life we discover how He coped with His darker feelings, & be encouraged in our darker times. We may think that Jesus had an advantage. since. He was God! But the power He used is available to us to call upon. We should not try to cope alone, but open our mind to God's Spirit within us. This help may come by empowering our thoughts, or by practical (may be medical) means.

Jesus faced up to His feelings, neither denying nor ignoring them. We can be encouraged when we realise that Jesus too encountered dark times & feelings. And always we can be assured that God is deeply involved with us in our response to the events we encounter. He is always alongside & within us, never leaving us to struggle if we seek His help. He is our Hope; our light in our dark hours. & bright hours.

GOD IS IN: POSITIVE FEELINGS

"Between the lines" of the Gospel we can find that Jesus' Life was not all doom and gloom. He must have been good company or people would not have crowded round Him to be with Him – He would not have attracted twelve men of very varying characters to live with Him day in and day out – or a group of women to leave their homes & cater for them on their travels. He was the welcome guest at Weddings and family meals, & invited to official lunches. He could tell a good story often with a subtle humorous twist. He could tease people & no doubt laugh with them. The children got on famously with Him. A positively likeable Man. This means that we can, & should, share our happy times with Him, aware of His Presence Sharing with Him our appreciation of laughter, of beauty, of companionship, & all the good and positive things of Life. which raise our feelings to enjoyment & happiness. Happiness & the deeper sense of joy are His gift to us. But we should not take them for granted. We must give thanks to Him & share our happiness; bringing happiness to other people. Knowing Jesus as the Companion of our joys will make it easier to contact Him in our darker feelings. He was also "a Man of sorrows & aquainted with grief".
God is sharing in our positive feelings.

GOD IS IN: SORROW AND REGRET

Isaiah the prophet foretold a Messiah as a
leader who would be "a man of sorrows and
acquainted with grief" (Isaiah 53:3) — This vision
was fulfilled in Jesus __ As well as happiness
He experienced the difficulties, & dark feelings
of all Humanity.   For example:
Jesus expressed the sorrow of frustrated
hopes & dreams as He mourned over the
blindness of the people of Jerusalem who refused
to recognise Him as Messiah (St. Matthew 23:37)
He wept tears of sympathy with the family &
friends of Lazarus who had died (St. John. 11:35) __ It
would seem that Jesus had to cope with the death
of Joseph, His mother's husband. (He is never
mentioned in the Gospel after Jesus was 12 years old)
We all experience sorrow, for many reasons
& at many depths ... disappointment, lost hope,
death of loved ones, job loss & such like __ We
can find our comfort in the knowledge that
in Jesus God has been through it too. So we
know sorrow is a natural part of human life.
Maybe surprisingly, sorrow can draw us closer
to God! ... if we allow Him into our feelings,
remembering that He knows how we feel.
For however broken-hearted we are Jesus has
felt it too, however low we feel Jesus knows
that too. God will always be there for us
to find in our darkness, our sorrow, our
regrets.

"I WILL HOLD THE CHRIST-LIGHT FOR YOU IN THE NIGHT-TIME OF YOUR FEAR"

GOD IS IN: <u>FEAR</u> AND PANIC

Jesus surely was afraid— even terrified— as in the Garden of Gethemane He faced the certainty of crucifixion... the most agonising death invented by mankind. "Watch with me" He begged His disciples, not wanting to face His fear on His own — "Take this cup from me" He begged His Father-God. The cup symbolising the acceptance of the blood He would shed... the blood of sacrifice for atonement. The blood of the death He must die if He were to show Humanity that Evil does not have the final victory. Jesus would show His enemies that He would accept their death-sentence, but defeat their power by rising back to Life. But first came the mental & physical terror of torture, & a horrendous death. Yes, Jesus knew fear. The depths of fear: sheer panic (St. Mark 14:34 ff). And we feel fear too. From "butterflies" of slight nervousness, to the utter panic of feeling we do not know how to cope; & the paralysing fear of fear; & the terror of dangers known & unknown. Our minds are overwhelmed, our pulses race, our stomachs churn.... how can we endure it? Jesus knew all this. He cried out to God, & so can we— Yet God did not change events for Jesus... He sent Him inner strength and courage (St. Luke 22:43/44). We can hold on, in our worst fears, to the knowledge that in the innermost, worst depths we are not alone. God is with us in our fear.

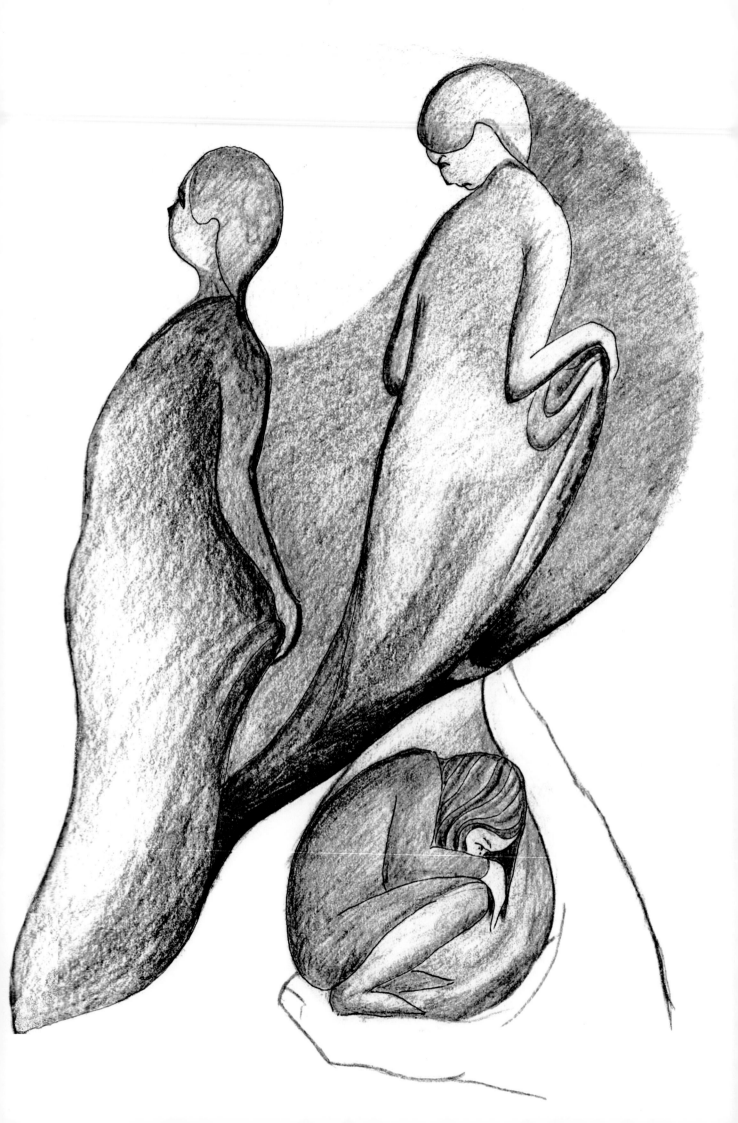

GOD IS IN: REJECTION & LONELINESS

Isaiah the prophet, foretelling the Messiah said: "He was despised, & rejected by men" (Isaiah. 53:3) From cradle to grave Jesus was rejected. Hearing of His birth King Herod rejected an apparent royal rival. With His parents fleeing to Egypt Jesus would have been aware, as babies are, of their fear — Then many times during His ministry the Jews turned on Him threatening to stone Him & trying to kill Him (St. John. 8:59 & 10:31) — Time & again the authorities rejected His claims (St. Luke. 22:2) until finally they arrested Him — Rejected again & again: by fellow countrymen, Jewish rulers, even His friends. Judas betrayed Him (St. John 13:2) Peter denied knowing Him (St. Matthew 14: 67-69) — The rest of the Twelve apostles "forsook Him & fled; so He must have thought they too had rejected Him (St. Mark 14:50) — Betrayed, denied & deserted; the final rejection, from the crowds who had once acclaimed Him, bawling for His death: "Crucify him!"   Not many of us will experience such rejection, but many will know the awful isolation of bullying; of being 'sent to Coventry'; made to feel unwelcome, unwanted. Maybe of being jeered at for some disability, or 'put in our place' by a superior. Many forms of rejection. The hurt is utterly demoralising: one wants to curl up & hide.   But remember Jesus. God knows, He still loves us, wants us; will come to comfort us, when we cry out to Him. We are not alone, in our innermost Self. God is there with us in our rejection, in our loneliness.

GOD IS IN: <u>DEPRESSION</u> AND DESPAIR

Depression is like a great dark cloud which descends & envelopes ones mind. It seems to blot out all logical thought, all hope, all ability to reason. At its worst it brings on despair, when one feels trapped in the misery. Jesus knew all this as He walked to the Garden of Gethsemone, & wrestled in prayer. (St. Mark. 14:34/35) (St. Luke. 22:44 & St. Matthew. 26:38) He knew Judas had gone to betray Him. He knew crucifixion awaited Him. He probably felt He had failed as a teacher. He knew their spiritual blindness (St. Luke. 24:25) In the Past people regarded depression as a sign of weak character, saying: "pull yourself together". Any suggestion of a sick mind was seen as insanity — only the body could be ill.
Jesus was not weak or insane; yet He plumbed the deepest depths of depression & despair... even sweating so that it poured off Him like great drops of blood.   This knowledge of Jesus' suffering can help us, even in our darkest hours. There is a strange companionship in shared experience, even of suffering. From it can be found the courage to endure — The tragic alternative would be suicide. We must never despise or condemn those taking this way out of, to them, unendurable suffering. "There, but for the grace of God, go I". (Oscar Wilde) It was not any easier for Jesus. He endured by calling on the strength of God (St. Luke. 22:43) — In depression & despair God is. there with us.

GOD IS IN: ~~FRUSTRATION~~ & ANGER

Stress is caused largely by Frustration. It is the
reaction to barriers in our life.   They may be
actual geographical barriers leading to "road-rage".
More likely it is in our personal life......A hope
dashed, promotion passed over, a plan
aborted, a dream unfulfilled, a suggestion
rejected, an idea repulsed, an attempt that
failed___ Frustration can explode into ANGER
& we hit out in words or action ... Which
usually causes more problems! It is wiser
to find a way round the cause, or remove it.
Jesus knew much Frustration! People following
Him for what they could get, rather than learn.
(St. John 6:26) His brothers rejected His message (St. John 7:5)
His personal friends didn't fully understand Him,
(St. John. 14:9)___ He was misunderstood, His hopes
dashed, dreams unfulfilled, rejected, repulsed,
left wondering if He had failed (St. John. 12: 37/38). His feelings
came to a head in the Temple, the holy centre of
worship, the "house of prayer (St. Mark. 11: 15-17)
Here creatures were bought for sacrifices, but
the sellers cheated people over the exchange
rate of special coinage. The worshippers were robbed.
To Jesus this symbolised His apparent
failure to put across His message... He made
a stand! Released doves & scattered the money.
No one was hurt, but He had made His point,
& dispersed His frustration in a positive way.
So God understands, He is there for us to calm
our frustration & show us a positive solution.

GOD IS IN: SUFFERING AND PAIN

Body, mind, spirit – can all be wounded. Can feel the burden of suffering, the agony of pain. Jesus must have suffered many times, in mind & spirit. We are told that He "groaned in spirit" (St. John 11:33) when He joined those who were mourning the death of Lazarus. Was it the effort required to raise the dead back to life in the face of their lack of hope or trust? But we think of His greatest time of mental & physical suffering being during the last 24 hours of His Life.

The Roman scourge was made of thongs of leather pierced with sharp metal bits. It tore the flesh. The sentence was usually 29 lashes; & Roman soldiers were not inclined to be gentle. They beat His back. Crucifixion was death by slow suffocation. With the weight hanging on the nailed hands, the throat was constricted & choking. The chest stretched wrenching the lungs & heart. Naked, exposed to heat & flies – it was not just pain. It was slow torture of body & mind. We all experience pain – from the small scratch to the splitting migraine; the slow pain of spreading cancer; the heartache of a bereavement. In one way or another we shall all suffer.

In our discomfort or our agony we can still seek the endurance of God to help us to endure. He is there for us, in our pain.

GOD IS IN: ~~ANXIETY~~ AND STRESS

Was Jesus cool, calm & collected all the time? He may have had a central core of Godly peace, but humanly speaking He was in many stressing situations. Was it likely that He was anxious before He changed water into wine in Cana? It was His first miracle... so maybe. He did hesitate. Confronting the antagonism of the Priests & authorities He would surely feel anxious, even though He knew He was in the right. But most of all, after His arrest...... He was physically rushed hither and thither: from the Sanhedrin court to Pilot, to Herod, back to Pilate ..... hit; spat upon; derided; cross questioned; challenged; dragged along by His roped wrists. All prior to scourging and final condemnation with the crowd screaming for His blood. Although He knew this was His destiny, did He wonder how He could cope? how He could endure?...With His body being strained to the uttermost, & His mind reeling. When we are worried and anxious about things the stress on body & mind can become overwhelming. How are we to cope? Inside us, as inside Jesus, God is present.... His dove-like Spirit of peace is there. Our minds can be turned to Him, as Jesus must have done. God is there in our anxiety, our stress. He is waiting to help us cope.

GOD IS IN: HOPE AND HOPELESSNESS

"There is always hope" we say — Perhaps it is the one feeling that can bring a little light into the dark times in life.... That can draw you upward from the depths of unhappiness. Without hope the hard times might well defeat us — But sometimes it seems all hope is lost. We feel hopeless because we don't know which way to turn to solve our problems, or how to rise above our negative feelings, & hopelessness — Jesus seems to have had endless hope in face of so many difficulties — Until perhaps that last brief moment on the cross when He cried: "My God my God, why have you forsaken me?" Somehow feeling cut off from God — But then hope returned. He realised God had not left Him alone .... It was just that as Son-of-Man He felt the separation of humanity from God — His ministry was ended: "It is completed" — God was no longer incarnate in Him: "Into thy hands I commend my spirit" — He experienced the awfulness of being without hope, but as He cried out to God hope returned. Hope in the completeness of God's wisdom being stronger than our failures. Hope is essential. Hope in God's presence with us, & in us, helping us through even our worst difficulties. When all hope seems lost to us... even then God will draw us to Him, & hope will spring up again — Hope will resurrect our positive feelings.

GOD
IN

EPILOGUE

In Part 2 I have tried to discover wherein Jesus experienced the same emotions & feelings as we do. I think He did; & I have referred to some of the occasions when this happened. I have tried to represent these moods in abstract pictures & through colour. I hope these illustrate that when we go through positive experiences, God shares these. And..(importantly).. when we are overwhelmed by negative feelings & all seems "darkness", & we may even feel distant from God – in actual fact He is very close to us. Because Jesus suffered what we suffer He shows us that He takes part in our 'lows' as well as our 'highs'. I believe that God became part of our human condition partly to show us what God is like. In doing this He has also shown that He is as much involved in our feelings as we are! He created our emotions as part of our human-ness.... there is nothing wrong in any of our negative feelings. They are a natural God-given part of our nature, just as are the positive feelings. Feelings are the body's way of expressing emotions. By becoming incarnate as Jesus God says:" I am with you always"... in all ways.

This has been a hard part to do because it has involved negatives that one would rather not examine closely. But it has also been strangely reassuring.

CONCLUSION

Is there a Conclusion?   I do not know.
In the Introduction (pages) I set out to try to
discover more about the personality & nature
of God, as revealed by Jesus: God-in-Man - in
His Life & teaching.   I discovered that He is,
beyond all else, infinite & mysterious!
I have tried to express in words & pictures
the things I have learned. A personal viewpoint.
I do not know why this had to become a book.
Now the book is full. There is no room for more.
But I am certain there is much more!

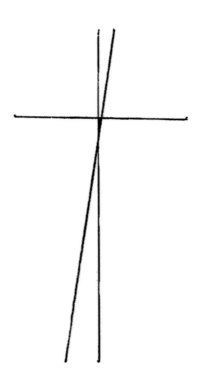

AN END MAY BE A BEGINNING

with thanksgiving & praise

INDEX